A Menu of Memories

Ted Morgan

First published (Paperback) in the UK in 2021
Violet Circle Publishing, Manchester, England, UK.

ISBN: 978-1-910299-32-6
Digital ISBN: 978-1-910299-21-0

Text Copyright © Robin John Morgan 2020.
Cover Illustration 'The Face of the Future' © Rin Zara Morgan 2020.
Cover background, digital images, and design. © Rin Zara Morgan 2020

All rights are reserved: no part of this may be stored in a retrieval system, reproduced or transmitted by any means, electronic, mechanical, photocopying, or otherwise without the prior written permission of the publisher, in accordance with the terms of licenses issued by the Copyright Licensing Agency.

All characters and scenarios in this publication are fictitious, and any resemblance to real persons, living or dead, is purely coincidental.

British Library Cataloguing in Publication Data.
A catalogue record for this book is available from the British Library.

All paper used in the production of this book are sourced only from wood grown in sustainable forests.

www.violetcirclepublishing.co.uk

Dedicated to
All who have added colour to my life
My family and my Friends

    This is my fourth book of poetry and is the usual mix of poetry about my observations on life, nature, and people, some humorous and also a few tinged with sadness. I am now 83 and retired 26 years ago after over thirty years nursing in both the general and psychiatric fields. I have seen great changes to the way of life since my childhood in the 1940's. As with most young men I had to do compulsory military service and I served in the Royal Air Force as a medic. I also was a member of a Mountain Rescue team for 20 years.
    I have filled my retirement with travel and woodwork, which I have sold at craft shows all over the north of England assisted by my late wife. With my advancing decrepitude I now spend most of my time writing, gardening, and fly-fishing.
    A number of these poems were written during the Covid outbreak of 2020
    I hope that you enjoy this small volume.
    All the royalties from my books go to the Bolton Hospice.

Butterflies

You see them when the sun comes out,
But never in the rain,
A fluttering flash of colour,
Their bright wings do proclaim,
Their names are very varied,
Painted Lady and Peacock,
But the Small White does damage,
To your newly planted crop,
The Red Admiral and the Tortoiseshell,
Are common ones you see,
But the Common Blue and Holly Blue,
Have not been seen by me,
Yellow Brimstone butterfly coloured like the sun,
The Marbled White, is black and white,
And not often come upon,
The Meadow Brown and Speckled Wood,
Roam meadows near and far,
Feeding on the nectar that's in every swaying flower,
This plethora of colour you see in summer's languid haze,
Before they mate, pupate and die,
Which ends their flying days.

Ode to my Garage

My car has some disturbing traits, as it reaches middle age,
No longer nice and shiny its colour drab and grey,
It's developed a kind of rattle, when on even roads it roams,
Which gives me palpitations and makes my wallet groan,
I'll have to take it down, to the grease monkeys at my garage,
To see what damage has been done that's left my car so ravaged,
A smiling face and breath intake, show's me I'm in a fix,
But first we have to ascertain, the true nature of the glitch,
We've got to drop the engine, gear box and the clutch,
Just to see the problem, it will not cost too much,
We know you have deep pockets, because of all you've spent with us,
Just to see you turn into here, gives all of us a buzz,
Its caviar for dinner, cream cakes and ice-cold beer,
From the profit that we make, as you drive your car in here,
You guys are all so helpful when divesting me of cash,
I'm reduced to bread and water, can't afford a restaurant bash,
My car emerges gleaming, with an engine ticking over,
But I am left with pockets bare, whilst the mechanics are in clover.

Messages

In uniform and pill box hat, a telegram boy in a country at war,
The bringer of all kinds of news, written in such short terse terms,
Missing in action, the message says, or we regret to inform,
This was as far as some recipients got, there in print the dreaded message,
The sender could not comprehend, the devastation caused by so few words,

A soldier fighting on the front, sees a letter from the one he loves,
But a Dear John letter in the envelope, turns his world upside down,
 Far from home and isolated, no chance to talk, what message can he send?
His love has gone, and he is left distraught and angry,
He must carry on and fight or maybe die, for what?

Times have changed, messages now go chasing round this cyber world,
We communicate by text, abbreviated in a language not understood by many,
Messages of joy, it's a boy! It's a girl! Congratulations!
Or to tell when we will arrive or depart, an airport or station,
 Instant messages now intrude into our life, no time to relax, we must tell all!

Those short messages, are they truly what we meant to say,
Or have we lost the ability to write at length, long descriptive missives?
Text messages are at times devoid of explanation, they are just plain facts,
Conversation, is the way to pass our happy or sad messages.
Is this an art that will be lost in the future, or will we talk by text?

The Geriatric Valentine

I'm just an aging Valentine,
Lothario I am not,
My hair is now greying,
But Dandruff I've not got,
My poor old back it aches a bit,
When I try to bend too low,
And my hearings not up to much,
So people, please talk slow.

My brain it's rather muddled,
Senior moments I have many,
And my water works they plague me,
So I often "spend a penny,"
I get a little tongue-tied,
When I'm questioned by a lass,
And I am embarrassed by my rear end,
As it discharges excess gas.

My intestinal rumbles are so loud,
That all around can hear,
And distracts adjacent diners,
When in restaurants I appear,
I order meals I fancy,
But problems then ensue,
My false teeth they go walkabout,
When steaks I try to chew.

I've aches and pains in both my feet,
My fingers and my head,

Which causes me some problems,
As I try to climb in bed.

Seduction does not come easy,
I forget what I'm about,
And all of my old girlfriends,
When I call, seem always to be out,
Please find me a lady,
That will put up with my aging traits,
For this aging Geriatric wants a loving female mate.

New Year

We sit around and wonder what things we're going to change,
When the clock it does strike twelve, our lives we rearrange,
It seems to happen every year, but very little changes,
Our resolutions come to naught, when our routine re-engages,
Our waistlines stay extended, we think of exercise,
But staying on the sofa, remains central to our lives,
Our masterplan for New Year, remains static on the shelf,
We pour ourselves a whisky as we dream of a "new self"
But do we have to change at all? Is our life so bad?
We have a loving family, and strong friendships make us glad,
So, let us try this New Year, to rejoice in what we have,
And count the blessings in our lives, so we never will be sad.

National Older Persons Day

On listening to the radio,
I had a great surprise,
It's National Older Persons day,
As from my bed I rise,
I did not know, why it's so called,
And when one qualifies,
For in my head I'm still eighteen,
My body tell me otherwise,
But then it got me wondering,
When do other folks get old?
I'm sure it's just your mind-set,
To stay young so I'm told,
I'll have a great big cream cake,
And a glass or two of gin,
To celebrate this old folk's day,
And the knackered shape I'm in.

Change

Our life consists of many changes, some we make ourselves,
Others are forced on us by circumstances, or dictated to us,
Many people resist change, because it creates uncertainty,
Or it alters our routine, causing personal stress,
Others embrace the prospects and challenges that change brings,
Yet in life, change plays an important part in our development,
We change constantly in our everyday lives, our clothes, our hair,
And even our minds when confronted with logical reasoning,
Our attitude to life is often modified by different experiences,
As we get older, we change in many ways, both physically and mentally,
Without change there can be no progress,
Without the challenges that change brings, life would be very dull.

It's a Car Thing

When I first started driving, a clapped-out Viva's what I had,
It was in the garage so much, it really made me mad,
I went and did a trade in, for a Peugeot 104,
But the darn thing it was like a sieve, with water on the floor,
A Mini that was new was bought, and it gave me hours of fun,
But I tried to teach my son to drive, in a tree it did run,
Next was the Allegro and what a tune it played,
But a grinding noise in the engine, sent it to its grave,
The Talbot Solara was, the next one that I owned
But after a brief time, the alloy engine I disowned,
The Metro next on the list, a good car of its type,
I drove it for a couple of years it lived up to its hype,
A brand-new Rover was the next, elegance sublime,
A drove it for a good few years before I called it time,
A Larda was the next one, a hatch back big and roomy,
But driving it was like a tank it made me feel so gloomy,
A Proton it was purchased, to craft shows it did travel
But then I saw a Waggon R, and with the salesman I did haggle,
I travelled round to many shows, good things of it was written,
But then my wife she fell in love, with a Berlingo made by Citroen
I now do drive this battered car, my wife alas has gone,
But her love for it, has got me hooked and so I soldier on

Christmas Cards

A ritual at Christmas that dates from Christian praise,
Is the sending of a Christmas Cards, to friends of bygone days,
Many you have not seen for years, from your environs they have fled,
But a card from them at Christmas time, shows that they're not now dead!
The themes of cards are many, from cribs to snowy freeze,
Ringing bells and mistletoe, Santa's sleigh above the trees,
But which one to send each person, a design that is just right,
To capture their persona, and when opened cause delight,
To many people on their own, a card brings Christmas joy,
It shows that they're not forgotten, by a favourite girl or boy,
Some comic cards are now sent, to people who are friends,
To raise a smile at Christmas or just to make amends,
For all the tricks that you have pulled, now the old year ends,
Advent is the season when we await the Christ child's birth,
And cards sum up this season of celebration joy and mirth.

To celebrate my good friend and fellow radio presenter Johnny Crook the Westhoughton Town Crier.

The Town Carier

He walks down Church Street likes a Toff,
With tricorn hat he likes to doff,
Red Coat, white breeches and some squeaky shoes,
With scroll in hand he doth amuse,
News for Howfeners here about,
His voice he raises to a shout,
Have no fear Johnny C is here?
He was a policeman in yesteryear,
But now as Howfens Bard delivers,
In a voice at times that cause a shiver,
His tinnitus inspired odes and verse,
But he, I'm told does not rehearse,
But memorises all his lines,
(But sometimes leaves a few behind,)
So, if you see him hereabout,
Do not ignore him, give him a shout,
Or listen to his verse, he will not bore,
On Howfen Radio, each Wednesday 2 till 4.

Easter

You walk into the supermarket, the isles are packed with goods,
It's Eastertime and all you see are Eggs in large bright tubs,
The place is full of Bunnies, and chicks and daffodils,
And all the men in marketing hope, to just expand your bills,
But this is not what Easter, is really all about
No mention of the cross of Christ and the redemption that it brings,
No Garden of Gethsemane, or betrayal of our Lord,
It seems so many people have cast these things aside,
And religion is a subject that so many can't abide.
The sorrow of Good Friday and the joy of Easter Day,
Are a measure of the path that Christians walk today,
I hope that you reflect on the message that it brings,
And the passion of our saviour which saves us from our sins.

The Interloper

My bird bath has been raided by a large and sinister bird,
It has frightened all the Sparrows, and the Blue Tits they are scared,
It swooped in last Friday and it seems to have taken over,
As it saunters round my garden midst all the grass and clover,
Its plumage it just glistens, feathers and beak are black,
And I rushed to the bird book, as recognition I did lack,
The regular birds, that I saw most every day,
All seem to have deserted me, and simply stayed away,
It seems it's a Raven that has graced me with its presence,
And with its regular bathing gives his coat a luminescence,
I wish it would return to its Tower of London home,
And allow my other residents to feed quietly on their own.

Spring Walk

You walk slowly down a country road, over a style and down a lane,
The gentle breeze in your hair, the meadow grass beyond compare,
And trotting gaily by your side, a fluffy dog that's keen of eye,
The sun high in the springtime sky, and wispy clouds go sauntering by,
The air is filled with buzzing bees and skylarks warble on the breeze,
The flowering chestnuts grace the scene, bedecked as if a regal queen,
And bluebells peep from forest glade, to spread a carpet, natures made,
This tranquil scene is all you need, to calm and sooth, and have fears relieved,
And for a little while at least, you look in awe at natures feast.

Spring Dawn

Mist rises slowly from the dew-soaked grass,
The dawn breaks slowly through the dappled trees,
Birdsong heralds the slow awakening of the day,
Whilst wispy clouds scurry across the red streaked sky,
A man walks slowly along the winding path across the field,
Deep in thought, enjoying this period of solitude,
Flowers raise their dewy heads towards the rising sun,
The first squirrels chase about the grass in search of sustenance,
Crows strut about, like military sentries,
The kestrel hovers in the sky looking for an early feast,
The peace and serenity of the early morning,
Heralds the challenges of the day ahead, for both man and animals.

My Memory Stick

Someone's pinched the memory stick that lay within my brain,
I know I'm getting on a bit, which causes some disdain,
But my stick it functioned perfectly as exams I did take,
I qualified with letters, which proved I was awake,
But as I've reached my dotage now, a malfunction has occurred,
My memory stick's gone walkabout, remembering's not assured,
Someone asks a question and the answer I should know,
But the memory sticks malfunction deals me a mortal blow,
I do feel kind of stupid, in my head I see the thing,
But the word for it I can't recall. my memory bells don't ring,
I've put my keys down somewhere, I know there in the house,
I vainly search in every room 'cos I know there hereabouts,
I leave the room to do a task, my mind is so assured,
But when I get to the other room, my task is now obscured,
I went a walk the other day, and a friendly face I saw,
Chatted on this and that, but of his name I was not sure,
Folks tell you of the joys of reaching your golden years,
But losing your memory stick, leads to frustration and some tears.

The Lonely Man

He sits near the phone, and hopes it will ring,
For someone, to just say hello,
He's been on his own now, for many a year,
So sad at what loneliness brings,
His past life was full, of excitement and joy,
Felt fulfilled, in a job that he loved,
With a wife by his side, and children as well,
He felt blessed by the good Lord above,
The kids fled the nest, but that was just fine,
His wife was the love that he craved,
Their retirement was grand, as they strolled hand in hand,
Down a beach on some wild coral strand,
But illness then took, the love of his life,
He walked behind her coffin in church,
Went home, to a house that was silent and still,
Not at all like his loved wife's domain,
Everyday tasks were now his to do,
But the ache in his heart still remained,
He knows he must try, as each day goes by,
To widen his view and his friends,
But still counts the cost of the love he had lost,
And loneliness is all that remains.

Drinking Vessels

We all use cups and glasses to quaff our tea or wine,
But shelves are used to store them all, before we go and dine,
But the many types of vessel we use for our daily tipple,
Has made me tabulate the forms, in this my drinking missal,
The feeding cup is in use when ill or still a tot,
But cups and mugs are what we use for drinks served piping hot,
The Sundae glass with shapely form, we serve, when ice cream is to hand,
But beer is in a tankard whilst at a bar we stand,
Brandy's served in balloon shaped glass, champagne in slender flute,
And sherry in a schooner is a drink you don't dilute,
A high ball glass for cocktails, a Quaich for single malt,
And liquors in a tiny glass as your taste buds it assaults,
A yard of ale is sometimes drunk when out on boozy parties,
But hangovers the next morning, make you feel not hale and hearty,
These myriad drinking vessels we all use throughout the day,
Ensure that we all use the one, that's correct in every way.

Heatwave

We're going to have a heatwave, or so I have been told,
The sun up in the heavens, is going to have some fun,
Instead of jetting off, to the Costa's or to France,
We're going to bake on loungers, in our gardens given the chance,
The supermarkets stocks, of sun cream have all gone,
And knicker drawers are ransacked, for Bikini's to put on,
Barbecues are set up, for eating burnt sausage, and baked spuds,
Whilst children play in paddling pools, blow bubbles from soap suds,
We all complain about the heat and rush to buy a fan,
But sold out notice in the shops distress us to a man,
A thunder storm may come to pass, as the hot and cold air meet,
And lightning flashes in the sky, serve up a photographic treat,
We Brits are not used to this thermal supernova,
And many bitch and moan, and hope it will soon be over,
So, settle down, enjoy the sun, get nice and pink or brown,
And enjoy your treat of sunshine, sit tight untill sundown.

Reading

How is it some people boast "I've never read a book,"
I'm sure at school they had to do, but now it's just a joke,
I feel so sorry for these people, they do not comprehend their loss,
To walk the lanes of literature and the many roads they'd cross,
Sat in your chair you travel, to countries of the world or space,
And learn of different lives, and reflect on the customs of each race,
Or else the myriad characters created in an author's mind,
A constant stream of people's lives is what we surely find,
They draw us into the tale they tell, its story, plots, intrigue,
And cast a spell upon us as we turn, the volumes many leaves,
Our minds they go on walkabout, from the stress of daily life,
As the writers gently guide us though their own imagined strife,
The happy hours spent reading have filled us with such joy,
And I still remember fondly, stories that I read, when just a boy.

Money Talk

Before we had the decimal we had just pounds, shilling and pence.
And a farthing was the smallest coin t'was there for all to see,
A halfpenny then followed, next up was the penny,
A large and very bulky coin so you did not carry many,
The threepenny bit was the next followed by the tanner,
Or sixpence as it was known, in the correctly speaking manner,
Our next coin was the shilling or "bob" as it was known,
And two of them made up a coin simply called the florin,
A half a crown was next in this panoply of coins,
And shillings five made a crown, not of the wearing kind,
Paper money it came next, the ten bob note for sure,
And twenty shillings made a pound our money now secure,
The odd one out in all of this, was a rare piece called a Guinea,
Twenty plus one shilling its value, but rarely used by many,
A Golden sovereign was a coin seen by very few,
The rich in vaults kept them, away from poor folk's view,
Now decimal coinage has made our maths easier to manage,
The maths involved in pounds, shilling and pence, made some people disadvantaged.

Menu

I go into a restaurant, the menu I pick up, but what I see confuses me,
Instead of neatly tabulated type of soup inscribed there on,
Soup of the Day I see, I have to enquire what it is, which is a pain to me,
The fish course is the next one, that causes more confusion,
Catch of the Day is all it says, a sardine, shark or tuna? I ask with trepidation,
A lemon sole is what I'm told, why is it not inscribed for my approbation.
The entrée is the next on list, a posh word for main course,
Instead of dishes typed on card, specials is what I see,
You have to go and look on't board to see what fares for thee,
Seasonal veg is next in line, they can't say what's on offer,
Why can they not write the veg, on menu's that they proffer,
Pudding is the last on't list, desert when talking proper,
At least these are written down, except the special offer.

The Fall

Morning mists, chilly dawn,
Falling leaves, dew-soaked lawn,
Watery sun high in sky,
Autumnal breeze as you walk by,
Flower heads droop, then they die,
Skeletal trees, leaves on ground,
Bedeck our countryside and towns,
Shorter days, night time chills,
But autumnal colours sometimes thrill,
Reds and golds russet browns,
Yellow tints this seasons crown.

Prior to joining the police force my friend Johnny Crook took a temporary job as a Bus conductor the only problem being, he suffered from car sickness since his childhood!

❦ Queasy Conductor ❦

Now Johnny is bold and fearless,
Atherton the town of his birth,
He came from a long line of seafarers,
Famous to the ends of the earth,
T'was Quarterdecks they paced upon,
With telescope's close to their hand.

John tried a voyage, on a boating lake,
But it did not go as he planned,
Six feet from the bank his stomach, he felt,
Was not his to command,
His head it spun, his colour changed,
And his breakfast fed the fish,
And some popped out to thank him,
For providing a real tasty dish.

His Mal de Mer was a problem,
When traveling in the back of dad's car,
For these nauseous journeys in childhood,
It seems were a permanent scar,
As a landlubber he worked in a garage,
Panel beating, welding and such,
But after a while he was restless,
So got a job as a conductor on't bus.

In uniform he looked so dashing,
His ticket machine gleamed in the sun,

But for john and his rebellious stomach,
His nightmare had just begun,
The lanes of the bus route were twisting,
And from side to side the bus swayed,
The green faced and sickly conductor,
It was to the good Lord that he prayed.

Each journey to him was a nightmare,
He was sick at the end of each run,
So his mates at the depot did tease him,
As his malady caused so much fun,
Stories are told of his exploits,
When battling his cursed mal de mar,
But he left and joined bobbies in Salford,
Patrolling the beats that were there.

◦ Gastropods ◦

They live deep in the greenery, out of sight and mind,
Slimy slithery gastropods, midst greenery they're confined,
They munch the flowers and foliage, leaving unsightly serrated edges,
And produce a myriad little ones that nestle under hedges,
In daytime they are sleeping whilst the mid-day sun does shine,
But come the night, you find them midst flowering Columbine,
Out from their daytime hideouts, advancing slimy hoards,
Attack the flowering borders, and climb the fencing boards,
Their friends the snails assist them, in this nightly task,
But to eliminate these creatures is I know a great big ask,
I've tried the pellets scattered round, gravel and slug traps,
And salting slugs every night, does cause them to collapse,
My fight it is unending, I hate their silver trails
But most of all I can say I loathe all Slugs and snails.

What's An App?

What's an app? A friend did say I had not got a clue,
So with my brian in top type gear, I said I thought I knew,
It's just a word with app to start, I smartly put him right,
And apple was just such a word, I thought myself quite bright,
His brows they crossed in disbelief, you are just wrong he said,
I'm sure there's more to it than that, and he just shook his head,
Well what about, appliance or even to appeal,
They start with app I said, they truly are the deal,
We were stood outside a mobile shop or cell phone in US,
We'll go inside and ask the guy I'm sure he will impress,
We went inside and asked him, he smiled at our consultation,
Then with a grin said, it's just an application.

Christmas Poem 2019

Symbols of advent are all around, cards in shops, joyous sounds,
People are crowding in markets and stores,
Buying the presents which tradition ensures,
Whilst on the streets of the city, the homeless are there,
Some drugged or drunk or just in despair,
One never knows the stories they tell,
Of breakup or heartache and illness as well,
We just walk on, our eyes do not see,
How troubled and lonely these people can be,
A few people at Christmas, disturbed by their plight,
Do offer a meal and a bed for the night,
Emulating the story passed down through the ages,
The baby, the stable, the visit of Sages,
Let's hope that the homeless, find ease from their plight,
And New Year brings secure homes for the night.

Six Years

Six years have passed, since I lost my dear Pat,
But my ache has not gone, and I'm so sure of that,
Each day I remember, the love that we shared,
And I look at her chair, now empty and bare,
My memories they tumble around in my brain,
A montage of photo's I will always retain,
Her smile is a memory I see every day,
Her presence in my home, never far away.

Winters

Skeletal trees, chilly morns,
Frozen grass, misty lawns,
Bird-song muted, air so still,
Distant mountains, snow on hills,
Wrapped up people, frozen breath,
Icy roads, Sudden death,
Days length short, long dark night,
Mood is low, no end in sight,
People long for winters end,
When with ice and snow they do contend.

Christmas Gifts

We all give gifts at Christmas time, but do we spend too much?
The season is not all about the cost of things and such,
We surely can give presents, that do not cost at all
If we just think about what we give, when we just make a call,
The visit to some lonely soul whose friends have all passed on,
To have a chat and cup of tea, to show they're not forgotten,
And make a vow to carry on and go that extra mile,
To bind the bonds of friendship which will leave them with a smile,
And any one that we have hurt, to say sorry and do mean it,
And repair the split, that caused the rift in our relationship,
These acts when feely given, are worth more that bars of gold,
For they display the ethics passed down from days of old.
So give to folks these priceless gifts, not purchased from a store,
They far out last any articles; of that I am so sure.

Christmas Time

Advent candles, Christmas cards, angel atop the tree,
Turkey, Sprouts and stuffing a feast, for you and me,
Christmas pud and brandy sauce, and a drink or two at least,
All go towards the yuletide joy, that fills our hearts with peace,
Sleigh bells jingle, church bells ring, carols that we sing,
Baubles hung on Christmas trees, presents that we bring,
The baby in the manger, over the stable is a star,
The wise men as they travel to the manger from afar,
Sheppard's watch the eastern star, surrounded by their sheep,
And angels watching over all, as a vigil they do keep,
This is the time of love and joy, of family and of friends,
To look back on the year that's past, and perhaps to make amends.

The Repair Shop

There is a programme on the BBC, where we bring our treasured things,
And experts in their chosen fields, mend the things we bring,
The memories that these things evoke, endow the possessors with such joy,
Most things are very are old and loved, a battered chair, a broken toy,
A pot that's shattered too, all remnants of a loved one's life,
Passed on to future family, form part of our life's glue,
We don't expect miracles but that is sometimes what we get,
Whilst skilful artisans, make our objects just like new,
"Thank you" seems hardly words enough, to express our heartfelt joy,
When are revealed the objects, we remembered as a girl or boy,
Grand ma's, Grandads, Uncles, Aunts, Mothers, Fathers too,
Remembered with such love and Joy, through objects that we knew.

Litter

Walk down any street in town detritus lying all around,
Empty cans and paper bags, chewing gum, discarded fags,
Plastic bags blow down the streets, resting in the neat hedgerows,
Some walk their dogs in parks and roads, but ignore the faeces they unload,
Some people say, that's not our job, as council workers we all do pay,
They should clean up the mess, but it's the littler dropper we should address,
Do they not care if streets are clean? A litter free and pleasant scene,
It seems at times to me, we have a throwaway society,
We can carry our litter to a bins repose, as unwanted items we dispose,
All should take pride in where they dwell, and littler droppers we should tell,
Do not drop detritus here, litter on streets must disappear.

Smartphone Zombie

Walking down the street one day, I spied an apparition,
For a man appeared in a daze, with no sign of inhibition,
His concentration total, of surroundings unaware,
His eyes were on his smartphone screen, as though in silent prayer,
Cars and people passed him, not a flicker of recognition,
His steps were slow and measured as though on a secret mission,
He is a modern Zombie, in towns they do abound,
Tripping up on pavements, hitting lampposts does astound,
This is a modern phenomenon, brought on by smartphone tech,
Peoples desire to keep updated, needs to be kept in check.

Cinema of Yesteryear

I remember when the cinemas lined every city street,
The Lido and the Odeon, Arcadia and Grand,
The commissionaire was stood outside in peaked hat and big coat,
Though what exactly was his job? he very rarely spoke,
The films they changed every week, and people went in droves,
Few houses had a T.V. and 'twas of the "Flicks" you spoke,
There were always two showings the first and second house,
But you could always sit through both, as they did not throw you out,
A newsreel started show, then cartoon and Movie B,
Then a break as Ice Cream Lady sold us Lions Maid, alas not cups of tea,
The big Movie was then shown with Hollywood stars galore,
No wide screen then, but technicolour made us shout for more,
At the end of the screening a union flag was shown,
We all stood still for "The Queen" then quietly left the show,
Saturday Mornings was the kids shows, ABC Minors to the fore,
 Hopalong Cassady and Roy Rogers, were favourites in days of yore,
The cowboys and Indians ensured we had plenty of games to play,
The cinema of yesteryear so unlike today.

Camelia

In the corner of my garden grows a tiny little tree,
It seems such a tangled mass, but it means a lot to me,
It started life in a pot and given with love to Mum,
But was planted in the garden, when its days indoors were done,
It blooms in days of winter when frosts and winds abound,
But my camelia flourishes and with flowers it is crowned,
It provides a haven for the birds who from its branches sing,
And bedecked in its red flowers, so much joy it brings,
It provides a lasting tribute to someone so greatly missed,
Who passed away many years ago, cruelly taken from our midst,
The joy it gives on sunny days makes my heart just sing,
Remembering all the happy times, and the memories that it brings.

Holocaust

The darkness descended,
The candle flame shone bright,
A flame of light and remembrance,
Illuminating the people gathered round,
The wax candle itself represents the millions slaughtered,
The melting wax the tears of the bereaved,
The wick our unending promise never to forget.

Acronyms

I am a rather ancient soul, some may say I'm staid,
I have embraced the modern world, on laptops I have played,
I have learnt to send e-mails text and tweets, in some, English is abused,
The thing that really gets me, is the acronyms they use,
Why do they have to shorten words or use disjointed Letters?
When English is so beautiful, that does not need such fetters,
I always answer messages with words all writ in full,
Or just ignore them if they are sent, in English they befoul,
So please send me an e-mail, with words all fully spelt,
Which will ease my anxious feelings, and replace them with calm svelte.

Reading Friends

We make our way across the town,
To where the books we read abound,
And meeting there each month, we see,
Our Reading Friends, alive, carefree,
Each month we do discuss our themes,
And recall books read in our teens,
It makes us re-evaluate our choices,
Spurred on by friends encouraging voices,
Our likes and dislikes on display,
Of which were unafraid to say,
But we also think of pastures new,
Our reading life could now ensue,
New authors to explore and delve,
As we search though the bookshop's shelves,
A marvellous way to share our pleasure,
Of books we read in days of leisure.

Another of my Covid 19 poems

Enforced Isolation

I am one of those poor people "At Risk" or so I'm told,
At over 80 years of age, you can see that I am old,
My watchtowers have been ordered and searchlights soon will follow,
My moat is being dug in haste with a digger I had to borrow,
I obtained an armoured helmet from a nearby castle keep,
My isolations total from that coronavirus creep.
I joined the hordes of shoppers and provisions I have plenty,
I'll dine on Rice and Pasta and packs of meat balls I have many,
My loo is packed with "bog rolls", soap and sanitizers,
lots of towels and sponges, and perfume atomizers,
My leisure time will be filled with jig saws and with books,
And showers and mud packs will ensure I keep my cherubic looks,
I'm ready for this period of enforced isolation,
To protect me from this malady's, deadly predilection.
How long I languish here is anybody's guess,
But I know that in my hundredth year, a card from the queen no less.

Mum's School

I've got myself a new job, thanks to Covid 19,
The kids have come home from their schools,
And lots of books and papers I have seen,
It seems that I have graduated from teacher training school,
And I did not even realise, my job switch was so cool,
I looked at all the lessons that my wards to me presented,
But teaching in a class from mum, was at times resented,
My addled brain I know was stressed, and thinking was contorted,
As my daring little charges, tried to get mums school aborted,
But I remembered how it was, when I went to school,
And laid down to my children, "Mum's classic golden rules,"
Sit quietly and speak only when your Mum speaks to you,
And if you don't do as she says, your playtime has gone too,
Tablet Time restricted if work is not done right,
And your "electronic dummy" tablets will be banned from you tonight
It's no use saying that "Miss", at school does not do that,
When Mums "n charge she will not tolerate, this kind of rebellious spat,
How long this situation will last, I really could not say,
But summer holidays are on hold, if "ball" they do not play!

Lockdown

At the zoo you look into the lion's cage, its paws they make no sound,
But now you are in lockdown, it's you going around and round,
The freedom that you value, was suddenly taken away,
And the government holds the whip hand, on how you spend your day,
The pandemic is the culprit that's caused your life to alter,
The stress and worry that you feel, cause your confidence to falter,
The kindly acts of strangers, make a difference to us all,
All staff in the hospitals have answered the clarion call,
You do not know how long, the situation lasts,
And all the "experts" can give you, are deeply varying forecasts,
I'm sure that we will triumph and defeat this deadly scourge,
Let's hope that we can find a cure, to get us back to work.

April Muse

Shafts of sunlight, April showers, birds arrive from foreign climes,
Nests are built and birds are singing, defending territories they have gained,
Tress in blossom leaves returning, skeletal winters garb transformed,
Daffodils 'neath trees in blossom, yellow trumpets everywhere
Heralding the bluebell carpets that will adorn the forests floor,
Days they lengthen, sunlight dazzles, nights from frosty slumber wakes,
Plants burst forth from winter's grasp, with shoots emerging from the earth,
Natures never changing pattern tis the season of rebirth,
So, April is the month that heralds the dawn of a new year's birth,
When nature's new beginnings, bring such joy to mother earth.

I first wrote these lines in 1985 as the lyrics of a Folk song sung by my Folk Group "The Ringley Folk". It tells the history of this valley and the people who lived and worked in the coal mines and mills of the area. They have now been reworked as a poem some 20 years later.

∽ *The Croal Valley* ∾

Round Bolton and Bury the Croal valley rolls,
The river it winds and canals carried coal
Some folk did weave and paper was made,
And at Wet Earth and Outwood men burrowed and slaved.

The old days are gone in the valley called Croal,
The ghosts of the people are gone with the coal,
The brickworks now closed and the locks are at rest,
The smoke and the grime's left a valley that's blessed.

The sounds of the worker up early each morn,
Have dwindled in the valley as their jobs have all gone,
The hiker and rider now plod on their way,
Where once barges and coal tubs ran every day.

The Nob Inn it stands where the canal it did rise,
The long flight of locks do not now surprise,
But out on the Vat Wastes the orchids now grow,
The valleys all green and the wild flowers show.

People once strived in this dim dismal place,
To eke out a living at loom and coal face,
The factories are gone and the barges are still,
And the valley now rings to the skylark's sweet trill.

My Walk

On my lockdown walk today I saw,
Arching trees in gentle breeze,
Rustling leaves I did perceive,
Dappled shade within a glade,
Birdsong trills, gave me a thrill,
Bluebells cover forest floor,
Soon to go and be no more,
Then wild garlic is in bloom,
Its pungent odour fills the air,
A walk to satisfy the soul,
And make one's heart just sing.

Covid Thoughts

I'm an 80 plus old person observing lockdown at this time,
I sit at home and wonder what has happened in this age,
My life has turned upside down, my freedom it has gone,
We observe this social distancing with all we chance to meet,
The little things are what I miss no hugs or close encounters,
No departing handshakes or kisses on the cheek,
Our social interactions are what makes us what we are,
No visiting the grandchildren to hear their cheery news,
And talking with our family with cups of tea or booze,
At home we occupy ourselves with mundane daily tasks,
The TV and the Radio and read a book or two,
But the thing that is missing, is the friendly human touch,
I hope that we soon get back, to some semblance of normality,
And people will recapture our human social geniality.

A Day in May 1945

A magical day, that day in May in nineteen forty-five,
The war at last was over, the German foe was crushed,
The relief on peoples faces was there for all to see,
Five years of war had changed their lives, they celebrate with glee,
Glad voices sang in unison those much-loved songs of hope,
Fathers, sons and lovers would return from far flung lands,
They would build a better Britain from the debris all around,
And look forward to the future of which they can be proud.

Relationships

What makes the basis of a relationship is often asked by some,
Love is a special bond that people write upon,
But other things are valid when two people tie the knot,
And are just as important so should never be forgot,
Trust is oh so special, between each person in the bond,
And honesty between the pair should be the aim lifelong,
Acceptances of their differences, they should never try to change,
Accept them with their faults don't try to re arrange,
Be loyal to each other no matter what life throws at you,
And support them in the bad times with the love that they are due,
Best friends they should always be with all the joy it brings,
And travel down the path of life accepting all these things.

A neighbour of mine is 89 years old and does seem to spend so much time sleeping.

ᔓ Mr Rip Van Winkle ᔕ

Now Alan's got a problem its cause is still not known,
But every time that he sits down, he sighs and starts to yawn,
His eyelids they feel heavy and his eyes start to close,
A warm and snuggly feeling fills his body and his toes,
It's no good watching T.V. and the radio's just as bad,
For no matter what he wants to watch he heads to the land of Nod,
He never heard the thunder, he never hears the rain,
He never hears the hailstone rattle the window pane,
On his armchair of repose, he sleeps the day away,
Until it's time to go to bed which neatly end his day,
Oh, how can he defeat it, how can he stay awake,
And watch the TV through the day and have the odd tea break,
It's not down to medication, or brain waves that are slow,
It's just the case his eyelids, are set to stop not go!

Sitting in my garden during the covid pandemic I was moved to write this verse.

ᎦᏳ My Covid Garden ᏣᎠ

I look up into a clear blue sky, no vapour trails do I espy,
No traffic noise as I sit, within my garden's calm ambit,
Birdsong from surrounding trees, drifts along on gentle breeze,
I revel in this tranquil scene, whilst Iris stand tall, and serene,
Nearby tees sway in time, Maple, Holly, new planted Lime,
Rose buds wait to burst into flower,
Leaves dappled from a morning shower,
Rosemary, Chives and Thyme, grow side by side beneath the Lime,
I sit in this tranquil haven, whilst on the bird bath sits a Raven,
I feel far away from Covids harm, safe, secure and quietly calm.

Branch Lines

In far off days the branch lines ran, that joined up country hamlets,
And steam trains puffed their way, around the English countryside;
Milk trains in the mornings stopped at every village station,
Each one adorned with flowering plants, a countryside oblation,
When Dr Beeching's Axe it fell, the little branch lines closed,
And silence reigned along miles of tracks, their cargo filled the roads,
Nature then took over, the cuttings filled with flowers,
Birds nested under bridges and perched on signal towers,
Foxes raced down rail tracks their cubs in close pursuit,
Whilst saplings grew along the tracks with intertwining roots,
A maze of bramble fortified these secret silent places,
Whilst willow herb encroached, all deserted desolate places.,
So thus, it was for many years, ignored by busy man,
But some then saw the potential, of where the tracks once ran,
Once cleared of all the railway tracks, and metaled paths created,
The hiker and the rider saw human travel reinstated,
So, people now can roam at will, down historic railway lines,
And enjoy the joyful freedom from their urban life confines.

I wrote this when my late friend Ann was diagnosed with terminal cancer.

Close Friends

Close friends we've been for many years, but Cancer now has intervened,
Unable now to roam at will, to restaurants to eat our fill,
Or laugh when strolling leafy bowers, by Manor house with large stone towers,
Whilst we discuss the flower beds, as birds they flutter overhead
Or gaze on things from bygone times, and marvel at the work displayed,
Crafted by skilled artisans, that bring such joy to modern man,
Our many memories we hold dear, bring us such deep and inner cheer,
Our friendship still strong and true, cemented by a bond like glue,
And if you falter, I'll be there, to be your rock in your despair,
So, take this proffered friendship hand, and we'll face the future hand in hand.

This happened when I was about 12 years old.

❦ Darkened Room ❧

Sitting in a darkened room, and through the window, pale dark moon,
The glowing coals in grate entombed, a plaid light fills the room,
The flames they flicker all around, patterns on the walls abound,
A radio from long ago, its oaken cabinet seems to glow,
"The man in Black" it's heard to say, I begin to feel some dismay,
As eerie music fills the room and enhances the air of gloom,
I sit frozen to my chair, engulfed by an aura of despair,
I strain to hear untoward sounds, my panic starts to feel no bounds,
I cannot rise from my chair, my mind tells me please beware,
The voice from the radio starts to tell, of man chased by hounds of hell,
Alone, afraid by flickering fire, my heart is racing, I perspire,
When suddenly the light switch clicks, I no longer feel transfixed,
My sister she came into the room, and in her hands, there was a broom
"Get up you lazy so and so, I have this room to clean, you know."

Vision

We all have a vision of what the future holds,
It starts when we are choosing our career,
The studies we have to do, to achieve our aim,
And the effort that is needed to succeed,

Our progress in our chosen field,
we chart each passing year,
And ambition is our vision and our guide,
We see the way ahead with some pitfalls and some dread,
And hope we will attain our stated goal,

We all view our world in such a personal way,
And to others it may seem we are off course,
But our views and path may change,
after discussion with a friend,
And our future vision we may rearrange.

We may not achieve our ambition and our aim,
As we travel the path of life to our goal,
But we all do have a vision,
of where our journey has to end,
Let us hope that we achieved our aimed for goal.

Comics of Childhood

It's funny when you think back, of the comics that you bought,
The Dandy and the Beano with Lord Snooty and his pals,
Desperate Dan with cow pies and the Bash Street Kids as well,
The drawings gave you pleasure in stories that they tell,
But as you gained in stature, your reading skills increased,
And my favourite ones as I grew up, gave me a reading feast,
The Adventure and the Rover were the ones I had to buy,
With the Wizard and the Champion, I never could pass by,
They were filled with sparkling stories, of characters heroic,
But then the Eagle came along I had to go and get it,
The Mekon and Dan Dare were my favourites of this genre,
And an Eagle badge upon your coat gave one a certain aura,
The movies then gave us character's, which now are commonplace,
With Batman and Superman, spiderman and such,
But comics I discarded when I found the joy in books.

Written when my grandchildren returned to school after lockdown.

ঞ Utopia ఴ

No more waring children, no telling tales to mum,
The six months of mayhem, the end at last has come,
No more home teaching; by stressed out mums and dads,
The sneaky digs and nudges, whilst purloining drawing pads,
The reason for this heavenly peace, this release from life so cruel,
Is that our little darlings have at last returned to school,
Our gin and tonics ready, with cream cakes on the side,
Positioned on a side table, our spirits fortified,
Lent back amongst the cushions of our favourite easy chairs,
Our head no longer whirls from the burden of childcare,
This idyll will last until about four pm,
Until our charges return home, to cause some more mayhem.

Covid Captivity

People are very sociable, human contact now distanced,
But the last few months of Corvid, has put this view to test,
Relationships at times are strained, when forced to live together,
Within a confined situation, which can cause some so much pressure,
You cannot go, just where you please, your life seems put on hold,
The Government gives you orders, on what you can, and cannot do,
A very Orwellian concept, to which resentment can ensue,
We also think of single folk, some of riper years,
Imprisoned in their houses by Corvid sickness fears,
Many feel abandoned by family and friends,
Few phone calls, and no 'puter' to skype call special friends,
No trips out for shopping, now delivered and just left,
No chance to chat, shake hands and hug, they feel at times bereft,
Let's hope that soon a fix is found so life it can resume,
With family, friends and grandchildren at peace within one room.

Autumnal Vistas

You step outside and feel the chill, the sky above is blue,
The trees around shine in the sun, leaves on the ground accrue,
The shimmering dew on the lawn appears, spiders' webs they gleam,
And on the trees the colours meld, in yellows, reds and greens,
The chestnut showers its conkers, in cases on the ground,
Gathered up by grateful squirrels, their winter food abounds,
Migrating birds, they gather, then depart, for far off lands and hills,
Whilst hedgehogs seek a haven, to sleep through winter chills,
Autumnal gales give rise to trees, stripped bare of leafy boughs,
And morning mists obscure the view, of our village church's tower,
This season is the time when we celebrate our harvest fare,
And offer our thanksgiving for the bounty that we share.

Seven Years

It's seven years since my dear wife Pat, left this earthy realm,
And left me at that time; alone and overwhelmed,
My life it changed forever, my soulmate now had gone,
And I just had to face each day; smile, and carry on,
 Memories are stirred, when treasured things are found,
That used to give Pat pleasure, and her joy it did abound,
But the secret ache within my heart, is not diminished by the years,
I miss her still each passing day, eyes clouded sometimes with tears.

Santa's Strike

Santa's got a problem his reindeers are on strike,
And suggest that he delivers toys on magic powered trike,
They want him to pay them extra, for working Christmas night,
Pluss waiting time on roof tops, when he finds the chimneys tight,
They say he drives them too hard as he flies around the globe,
And that he relies too much, on the light from, Rudolph's shiny nose,
They also want a limit on how much weight is in the sleigh,
And if he overloads it, he must pay them danger pay,
Dancers the shop steward and his rule book is to hand,
Formulated by the Union of Elves and Reindeers of Toyland,
Mrs Santa says that they are right, to ask for renumeration,
She says Santa is a tight old soul, and deserves their castigation,
This standoff had lasted through October and November,
But the thought of no flying reindeer sleigh, caused him to surrender,
So the boys and girls got presents on that special Christmas night,
And the reindeers got their extra pay via a union plebiscite.

❧ Christmas poem 2020 ☙

As Christmas time approaches, we look forward with some joy,
To times spent with our family, and food that we enjoy,
But this year has been so different, with its hardships and its fears,
A nationwide pandemic, who's losses have caused tears,
Our worlds been topsy turvy, restrictions been severe,
Proclaimed by the government, with advice made quite clear,
It's made us feel our life at times, lacks lustre and feels empty,
None of us will forget, the year of twenty, twenty,
We need to give some cheer, to the many who feel down,
And show some loving kindness, to remove their worried frown,
It does not mean big presents, ostentatious shows of wealth
But the milk of human kindness, from within our inner self,
So, visit, phone or talk, to folks, who are lonely or feel low,
Invite them for a chat and tea, in cosy fireside glow,
Show they're not forgotten in this fought and fearful world,
Let them see compassion, on the flag that you've unfurled.

Ode to our G.P.'s

A strange thing has happened in these covid-stricken times,
A species that we know so well, has burrowed underground,
They've not been seen by many, contacts are very few,
And they are guarded by a loyal band, of trained reception crew,
We try to penetrate their domain, by early morning calls,
But these are seldom answered or we're simply put on hold,
We're told that we can see the nurse, to answer all our ills,
And that a pharmacist will help us, with any queries about our pills,
But the person who we'd like to see, is rarely on display,
That's the G.P, we used to see, and talk to every day,
A Skype call or a phone chat is simply not the same,
A person in the flesh we want, other options are so tame,
Why have they gone to ground, disappeared and out of sight,
When other health professionals, mask up and seem alright,
Many folk feel abandoned, in this covid-stricken land,
And something approaching normal is what we now demand.

Red Poppies

We're proud to wear a poppy when November comes around,
It reminds us of the men who died in foreign battlegrounds,
But also it reminds us of the many who were maimed,
Who live a life now blighted, by the wounds that then sustained,
The British Legion's not forgotten them, and gives a helping hand,
When hardship and disaster assail them, and things don't go as planned,
So, all who buy the poppy help ex-service personnel,
Who served our Queen and county in roles that they excel,
Poppies red with centres black proclaim to all who see,
The gratitude we owe to those who served our country.

The Ladybird

When walking neath a summer sky a flash of red I did esspy,
And there it was, a ladybird, so elegant on flowering stem,
Bright red wings and spots of black, a royal diadem insect,
A regal insect to be sure, a queen of nature when mature,
Hiding out from winter chills, in large clusters mid forests and hills,
But come the spring they're all aglow mate, pupate, and then all go,
To help all gardeners for they feast, on aphid's, such nasty beasts,
The ladybird we all adore, and admire their beauty, of that I'm sure.

Summer Holiday

My wife has started to go on, about a holiday in the sun,
She states it's far too cold for her, to go to Bridlington,
It's off on planes to foreign climes, she says it's got to be,
But why the heck she has to go, and drag the likes of me,
I'd rather stay at home, and drink proper British ale,
Instead of all that foreign muck, with no body and it looking very pale,
I realize that it's no good, to shout and stamp and swear,
The misses take's no notice, at me tearing out mi hair,
So reluctantly I go on line to book a flight on't plane
But she'll have no cheap economy seats, it's first class, that's her aim,
She wants wide seats, free drinks, papers and silk napkins
Food served on real pot plates no plastic forks and knives,
And when it comes to hotels, my wallet starts to cringe,
No motels for my darling wife, it's a five-star luxury binge,
The hoiti- toity waiters with their noses in the air,
Those smooth lounge lizards that cause me such despair,
And talking of the of food, it's called Nouvelle cuisine,
One chip, two peas and a bite sized fish, not like the works canteen,
The other thing that gets me, is its foreigners wall to wall,
I suppose ill have to go with her our suitcase is in the hall.

Dragonflies

Go to any lake or stream in spring or in the summer,
And darting round a great display of iridescent colour,
With body long and swept back wings they perch on reeds and trees,
With gossamer wings the Dragonfly dances on the breeze,
As nymphs beneath the surface, they spend months down in the depths
Till they emerge, and then transform, via several amazing steps,
They bask in the sunshine till this process is complete,
Then spread their wings and fly to catch a passing insect treat,
Cultures throughout the globe, revere the dragonfly,
The Navajo worship it, in waters passing by,
Happiness and courage in Japan they indicate,
Whilst in China change and rebirth, their people celebrate,
To all who see the glittering sight, of dragonflies on the wing,
Hearts are filled with pleasure, and souls made to sing.

The Country Station

Walking down a country lane,
I saw a sight that caused me pain,
For there in all its glory stood,
A railway station now gone for good,
The pealing paintwork, broken door,
Ivy growing on platform floor,
A casualty of times long past,
When Beaching swung his fateful axe.

The flowerbeds now overgrown,
The trains on tracks no longer roam,
The station now alas neglected,
Where tickets were once collected,
By Station Master upright proud,
With authority he was endowed,
And all his domain clean and bright,
Station gardens to delight.

Steam trains hurtled through the station,
Speeding to far destinations,
Local trains stopped every day,
With goods from Wales or Galaway,
The ticket office all a- bustle,
Passengers with their cases struggle,
Porters trundled back and forth,
With goods destined for the north.

A golden age of the steam trains glory,
Mallard's record part of its story,
These images played in my mind,

As I observed what's left behind,
Now abandoned by modern man,
It's reached the end of its life span,
So sadly, I walked away,
But fond images in my mind still play.

Lancashire Grub

I had to Bolton the wheel,
For my cart to travel so far,
And I just hope the nuts Oldham,
As we travel to the fair.

I've got it filled with Chorley cakes,
And Wigan pies stacked high,
And I hope the folks of Bury,
Like my black puddings and will buy.

Our nearest city Manchester,
Has a tart named after it,
And Eccles cakes are world renowned,
For making you feel fit.

Chester buns where the Romans lived,
Were a great big hit,
And in the town of Howfen,
Westhoughton for the posh,
They made a flat type pasty,
Made of pork, a reet good nosh.

The cooks around our county,
Had much to be right proud,
Of all the food created,
And to our heritage endowed.

Modern Wasday Blues

It's Monday morning washdays here,
Different than in yester year,
Put the washing in the drum,
Press a button, hear the hum,
The drum rotates, soap suds appear,
And water sploshing I do hear,
No dolly tub and plunging posser,
Wringer turning made you fitter,
Gas boiler boiling all the whites,
Dolly Blue to make them bright.

Today we just press a button,
Forget this chore and ring a cousin,
And if we're posh a dryer too,
We can even go and clean the loo,
They do not scrub and peg outside,
Or if inclement dry inside,
It's Oh! so hard to wash today,
Or that is what some people say,
Modern washday is a breeze,
Machines now give us wasday ease.

ಸಿ The Teachers Read ಐ

Our teacher every day read to the class a chapter from a book,
It was The Exploits of Brigadier Gerrad by Arthur Conan Doyle,
Gerrad was an exciting, adventure loving scoundrel, a teller of tall tales,
We hung on every word the teacher read, about this bold Hussar,
But he left us wanting more, when his reading book he shut,
A new wooden library had been built near where I lived,
And the urge to know the stories end, lead me up the steps,
The counter scemed so very tall, on tiptoes I did stand,
And asked the lady standing there, how to join this special land,
I filled in a proffered form, my handwriting rather scrawly,
And the lady oversaw this act, her look was high and haughty,
Clutching my precious card, I looked at all the books,
And searched the titles for the book, my teacher had just read,
At last, I found the very book and headed for the counter,
Had it stamped, clutched it tight, ran home, and felt elated,
I sat and read my book that night, what joy when all was told,
And when my teacher read next day, the ending I exposed.

More Author's
From
Violet Circle Publishing

Mike Beale. (Children's Book)

Crumble's Adventures.
ISBN: 978-1-910299-06-7
Digital ISBN: 978-1-910299-08-1

Colin Smith (Play)

Heaven knows I'm Miserable Now
ISBN: 978-1-910299-16-6
Digital ISBN: 978-1-910299-23-4

Ted Morgan. (Poetry and verse)

Wordsmith's Wanderings.
ISBN: 978-1-910299-04-3
Digital ISBN: 978-1-910299-09-8
Peregrinations of the Wordsmith
ISBN: 978-1-910299-18-0
Digital ISBN: 978-1-910299-33-3
Silhouette Soldiers
ISBN: 978-1-910299-19-7
Digital ISBN: 978-1-910299-22-7
A Menu of Memories
Digital ISBN: 978-1-910299-32-6
Digital ISBN: 978-1-910299-21-0

Robin John Morgan. (Fiction/Fantasy/Slice of Life)

Heirs to the Kingdom.

Book One, The Bowman of Loxley.
ISBN: 978-1-910299-00-5
Digital ISBN: 978-1-910299-10-4
Book Two, The Lost Sword of Carnac.
ISBN: 978-1-910299-01-2
Digital ISBN: 978-1-910299-11-1
Book Three, The Darkness of Dunnottar.
ISBN: 978-1-910299-02-9
Digital ISBN: 978-1-910299-12-8
Book Four, Queen of the Violet Isle.
ISBN: 978-1-910299-03-6
Digital ISBN: 978-1-910299-13-5
Book Five, Crystals of the Mirrored Waters.
ISBN: 978-1-910299-05-0
Digital ISBN: 978-1-910299-14-2
Book Six, Last Arrow of the Woodland Realm.
ISBN: 978-1-910299-07-4
Digital ISBN: 978-1-910299-15-9
Book Seven, Bridge Of Sequana.
ISBN: 978-1-910299-17-3
Digital ISBN: 978-1-910299-20-3
Book Eight, The Circle of Darkness.
ISBN: 978-1-910299-26-5
Digital ISBN: 978-1-910299-29-6

The Curio Chronicles.

Part One, Abigail's Summer.
ISBN: 978-1-910299-27-2

Find out more about our authors and their books at

www.violetcirclepublishing.co.uk

Violet Circle Publishing Manchester UK

www.ingramcontent.com/pod-product-compliance
Lightning Source LLC
Chambersburg PA
CBHW070044230426
43661CB00005B/750